Kerplunk!

by Craig Hammersmith

Content and Reading Adviser: Joan Stewart
Educational Consultant/Literacy Specialist
New York Public Schools

 COMPASS POINT BOOKS

Minneapolis, Minnesota

Compass Point Books
3722 West 50th Street, #115
Minneapolis, MN 55410

Visit Compass Point Books on the Internet at *www.compasspointbooks.com*
or e-mail your request to *custserv@compasspointbooks.com*

Photographs ©:
Visuals Unlimited/Joe McDonald, cover; DigitalVision, 5; Index Stock/Image Ideas, 7; Visuals
Unlimited/Jack Dermid, 9; Two Coyote Studios/Mary Walker Foley, 11; PhotoDisc, 13; Two Coyote
Studios/Mary Walker Foley, 15; Visuals Unlimited/Joe McDonald, 16; PhotoDisc, 17; Visuals
Unlimited/Rod Kieft, 18; Two Coyote Studios/Mary Walker Foley, 19, 20, 21.

Project Manager: Rebecca Weber McEwen
Editor: Jennifer Waters
Photo Researcher: Jennifer Waters
Photo Selectors: Rebecca Weber McEwen and Jennifer Waters
Designer: Mary Walker Foley

Library of Congress Cataloging-in-Publication Data

Hammersmith, Craig.
  Kerplunk! / Craig Hammersmith.
      p. cm. -- (Spyglass books)
Includes bibliographical references (p.   ).
  ISBN 0-7565-0236-5 (hardcover)
  1. Pond animals--Juvenile literature. [1. Pond animals.] I. Title. II. Series.
  QL146.3 .H355 2002
  591.763'6--dc21

                    2001007337

Contents

Welcome to the Pond!

Plop! Splash! Kerplunk!
Ponds are home to
many different animals.
Some swim in
the *shallow* waters.
Some eat plants that
grow in the pond.

4

Did You Know?
Many plants can grow in a pond because sunlight can shine down through the shallow waters.

Insects

Insects live in or around a pond.

You can often find dragonflies at a pond. Dragonfly females lay their eggs in water. The young dragonflies live in water until they become adults and grow wings.

6

Dragonfly

Did You Know?
Young dragonflies breathe in the water using *gills*.

What Is a Mud Puppy?

Mud puppies live in or around a pond.

A mud puppy isn't a puppy at all. It is an animal that hatches from an egg in the water, and then lives on land when it is an adult.

8

Mud puppy

Did You Know?
Mud puppies are black, brown, or gray to blend into their surroundings. This helps them hide and keep safe.

Something's Fishy

Fish live in a pond.

If you look closely,
you might see a minnow.
Minnows are small and
blend into the background.
Minnows are often food
for larger fish.

10

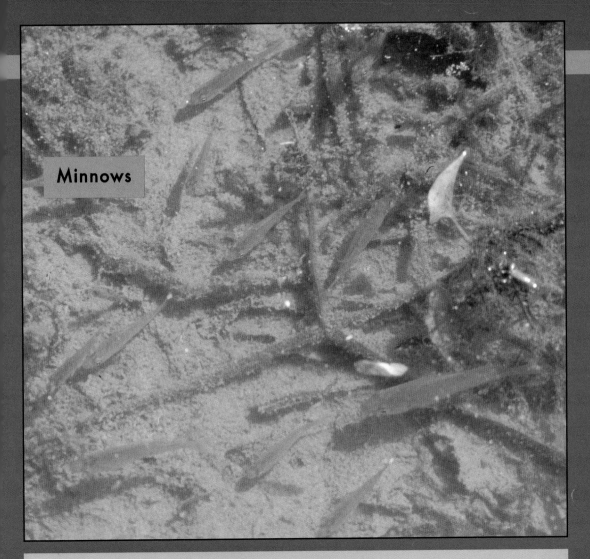

Minnows

Did You Know?

In cold weather, fish can live under the pond's ice. They breathe the air in the water that is trapped under the ice with them.

Frog Friends

Frogs live in or around a pond.

Female frogs lay their eggs in the water. The eggs hatch as tadpoles, or young frogs.

Frog on a lilypad

Did You Know?
A frog's legs help it jump on land. Its webbed feet help it swim in water.

Turtle Times

Turtles live in or around a pond.

You can often find turtles at ponds. They spend lots of time in the water, but they rest in sunny places to warm up.

14

Turtles

Did You Know?
A turtle's shell is its house.
The hard shell protects
the turtle's soft body.

Bird-Watching

Birds live at a pond.

Birds come to ponds
for the water and the food.
The great blue heron can
stand completely still in
the water until it spears
its meal with its bill.

Heron

Geese

Did You Know?
Canada geese and wild ducks often stop at ponds for food and rest during their *migration*.

Busy as a Beaver

Beavers live in a pond.

In fact, beavers make ponds!
They cut down trees
with their huge front teeth.
Then they build **dams**
and **lodges**.
A dam blocks up the water
and makes a new pond.

Beaver

Beaver lodge

Did You Know?
The entrances to beaver lodges
are below water!
Beavers build ramps that lead up to
the living area above water.

Fun Facts

Many ponds have turtles. Did you know the first turtles lived during the time of the earliest dinosaurs?

Modern turtle

These minnows are very small fish, but there is a kind of minnow in India that is 9 feet long.

Mud puppies are called "mud puppies" and "water dogs" because people once thought they barked like dogs!

Dragonflies can't fly when their wing muscles are cold.

Glossary

dam—something that stops water from flowing, causing it to back up and make a pool

gills—parts of an underwater animal's body that let it breathe oxygen in the water

insect—a small, six-legged animal

lodge—a beaver's home, built of trees and mud in a pond

migration—moving from one place to another at certain times of the year to find food and raise young

shallow—something that is not deep

Learn More

Books

Hickman, Pamela, and Heather Collins. *A New Duck: The Life Cycle of a Bird*. Buffalo, N.Y.: Kids Can Press, 1999.

Hickman, Pamela, and Heather Collins. *A New Frog: The Life Cycle of an Amphibian*. Buffalo, N.Y.: Kids Can Press, 1999.

Holmes, Anita. *Insect Detector*. New York: Benchmark Books, 2001.

Web Site

UK Online
http://web.ukonline.co.uk/conker/pond-dip/

Index

GR: G
Word Count: 250

From Craig Hammersmith

I like to camp in the mountains near my Colorado home. I always bring a good book and a flashlight so I can read in the tent!